God's Little Instruction Book

Class of 2002.

This book is a special gift to:

Lili Zhang

From:

Mom - Anne Yurkewich

Date:

April 26. 2002.

Encouragement
for the
Heart

Christian
Art
Gifts

ENCOURAGEMENT FOR THE HEART

Christian Art
PO Box 1599
Vereeniging
1930
South Africa

Designed by Christian Art

Christian Art has made every effort to trace the ownership of all quotes and poems in this book. In the event of any question that may arise from the use of any quote or poem, we regret any error made and will be pleased to make the necessary correction in future editions of this book.

ISBN 1-86852-591-0

Printed in Hong Kong

00 01 02 03 04 05 06 07 08 09 – 10 9 8 7 6 5 4 3 2 1

Encouragement for the Heart

These three remain: faith, hope and love.
But the greatest of these is love.
1 CORINTHIANS 13:13

~

Where there is charity and wisdom, there is neither fear nor ignorance. Where there is patience and humility, there is neither anger nor vexation. Where there is poverty and joy, there is neither greed nor avarice. Where there is peace and meditation, there is neither anxiety nor doubt.
ST. FRANCIS OF ASSISI

~

"Do not be afraid, O man highly esteemed,"
he said. "Peace! Be strong now; be strong."
DANIEL 10:19

~

When at times you really feel lonely and
discouraged, talk to the Lord. He walks the
road ahead of you. He supports you on all sides.

~

Greatness of soul consists not so much in soaring high and
pressing forward, as in knowing how to adapt and limit oneself.
MICHEL DE MONTAIGNE

~

I know that there is nothing better for men than to be happy and do good while they live. That everyone may eat and drink, and find satisfaction in all his toil – this is the gift of God.

ECCLESIASTES 3:12, 13

Having faith and trust is having courage – courage to be human, the desire to be human and the strength to develop my humanity. And we can indeed trust, since trust is after all accepting that He conquered the threats of life.

JOHAN HEYNS

Forewarned, forearmed; to be prepared is half the victory.
MIGUEL DE CERVANTES

God alone is the light which shows you the way at night, and when you have perhaps lost heart you will find your lost courage in this light.
PHIL BOSMANS

Do not be terrified; do not be discouraged, for the Lord your God will be with you wherever you go.
JOSHUA 1:9

Never give up!
If adversity presses,
Providence wisely
has mingled the cup,
And the best counsel,
in all your distresses,
Is the stout watchword
of "Never give up."

MARTIN F. TUPPER

The secret of success is constancy of purpose.

BENJAMIN DISRAELI

Cast away care,
he that loves sorrow
lengthens not a day,
nor can buy tomorrow.

THOMAS DEKKER

~

Life has a way of breaking us, which means that we can never be the same again. But God is capable of changing our situation to such an extent that we can rise above our darkness and sorrow. And although we carry the marks of the cross, there is also something of the glory of the resurrected Christ in us.

WILLIE JONKER

~

Today well lived makes every yesterday a dream of happiness and every tomorrow a vision of hope.

FROM THE SANSKRIT

~

I have learned that success is to be measured not so much by the position that one has reached in life as by the obstacles which one has overcome while trying to succeed.

BOOKER T. WASHINGTON

~

It is good to know that everything in this world is but temporary. Everything passes. And the child of God can know for certain that heaven awaits him.

There is no failure except in no longer trying.

ELBERT HUBBARD

~

Their king will pass through before them, the Lord at their head.

MICAH 2:13

~

The Lord never expects the impossible from his children. None of us is perfect. Therefore it is not necessary to list your faults and become depressed. Now I know – some things may seem like disasters, but are in actual fact acts of mercy.

PHIL BOSMANS

~

Just as the cross and the tomb of Jesus were not the final word on Him, the darkness of our despair is not the final word on us if we faithfully wait on God.

WILLIE JONKER

~

I lift up my eyes to the hills – where does my help come from? My help comes from the Lord, the Maker of heaven and earth ... he who watches over you will not slumber ...

PSALM 121:1-3

~

Our greatest glory is not in never falling, but in rising every time we fall.

OLIVER GOLDSMITH

Never despair. But if you do, work on in despair.

EDMUND BURKE

~

People do not lack strength; they lack will.

VICTOR HUGO

~

The man who succeeds above his fellows is the one who, early in life, clearly discerns his object, and towards that object habitually directs his powers.

EDWARD BULWER-LYTTON

For a man's ways are in full view of
the Lord, and he examines all his paths.

PROVERBS 5:21

Have courage for the great sorrows of life and patience for the small ones; and when you have laboriously accomplished your daily task, go to sleep in peace. God is awake.

VICTOR HUGO

Doubt whom you will, but never yourself.

CHRISTIAN BOVEE

The Lord will guide you always; he will satisfy your needs ... and will strengthen your frame. You will be like a well-watered garden, like a spring whose waters never fail.

ISAIAH 58:11

Whether God has a hand in our pain we really do not know; what we do know for certain is that he takes our hand when we suffer.

DANIËL LOUW

Be not afraid of going slowly; be afraid only of standing still.

CHINESE PROVERB

Our doubts are traitors,
and make us lose the good
we oft might win,
by fearing to attempt.

WILLIAM SHAKESPEARE

~

We shall steer safely through every storm, so long as our heart is right, our intention fervent, our courage steadfast, and our trust fixed on God. If at times we are somewhat stunned by the tempest, never fear. Let us take breath, and go on afresh.

ST. FRANCIS DE SALES

~

They can conquer who believe they can.

RALPH WALDO EMERSON

~

When I am afraid, I will trust in you. In God, whose word I praise, in God I trust ... I will know that God is for me.

PSALM 56:3, 4, 9

~

Someone who has walked through the darkness of depression has developed a certain inner strength which makes him a wiser person, and has acquired wisdom which can carry him through the rest of his life. His priorities are confirmed afresh and this can turn life into a deeply satisfying experience.

MARIETJIE VAN ROOYEN

To dry one's eyes and laugh at a fall, and get up and begin again.

ROBERT BROWNING

~

If I cannot conquer my fear, but fall victim to it, the origin of my fear is no longer outside of me, but inside. Then I have become seriously ill and I need a physician.

JOHAN HEYNS

~

Excellent therapy against depression is to look away from myself and my problems, and then I will see the (often much more serious) problems that others have.

Whatever is true, whatever is noble, whatever is right, whatever is pure, whatever is lovely, whatever is admirable – if anything is excellent or praiseworthy – think about such things.

PHILIPPIANS 4:8

~

Genius is eternal patience.

MICHELANGELO

~

We need others to help us sort out our problems. Unfortunately, we are reluctant to make our weaknesses known to others. Everyone tries to hide his sins. The result is emotional disruption and depression.

The gem cannot be polished without friction, nor man perfected without trials.

Confucius

"Because he loves me," says the Lord, "I will rescue him; I will protect him, for he acknowledges my name. He will call upon me, and I will answer him; I will be with him in trouble ..."

Psalm 91:14, 15

Without faith a man can do nothing; with it all things are possible.

Sir William Osler

Throw away all ambition beyond that of doing the day's work well ... Live neither in the past nor in the future, but let each day's work absorb your entire energies, and satisfy your widest ambition.

SIR WILLIAM OSLER

~

Then they cried out to the Lord in their trouble, and he brought them out of their distress ... and he guided them to their desired haven.

PSALM 107:28, 30

~

It is no disgrace to start all over. It is usually an opportunity.

GEORGE MATTHEW ADAMS

The battle is not to the strong alone;
it is to the vigilant, the active, the brave.

PATRICK HENRY

~

As I am a Christian I may never be without hope.
Since Christ has already conquered all the stress and
anxiety in the world I can also do it – in his strength.

Perseverance is a gift of the Holy Spirit. It is hope for the future
which gives the believer the strength to persist until the race is run.

WILLIE JONKER

In this you greatly rejoice, though now for a little while you may have had to suffer grief in all kinds of trials. These have come so that your faith ... may be proved ...

1 PETER 1:6, 7

~

It is easier to resist at the beginning than at the end.

LEONARDO DA VINCI

~

When the clouds of depression close in around you, there are two things you can do: list your blessings and thank God for these. Sing Him a song of praise!

~

In my anguish I cried to the Lord, and he answered by setting me free. The Lord is with me; I will not be afraid. What can man do to me?

Psalm 118:5, 6

Never undervalue yourself. Believe in yourself. Believe that you can do your work well, and then make good. Never doubt yourself. Faith in one's self unlocks those hidden powers that all of us have, but that so few of us use.

Albert J. Beveridge

I have to – therefore I can!

He confirmed it with an oath. God did this so that, by two unchangeable things in which it is impossible for God to lie, we who have fled to take hold of the hope offered to us may be greatly encouraged. We have this hope as an anchor for the soul, firm and secure.

HEBREWS 6:17-19

~

The greatest mistake you can make in this life is to be continually fearing you will make one.

ELBERT HUBBARD

~

The journey of a thousand miles begins with one step.

LAO-TSZE

Sow a thought,
and you reap an act.
Sow an act,
and you reap a habit.
Sow a habit,
and you reap a character.
Sow a character,
and you reap a destiny.

ANONYMOUS

~

Virtue is bold, and goodness never fearful.

WILLIAM SHAKESPEARE

~

Surely the arm of the Lord is not too short to save, nor his ear too dull to hear.

ISAIAH 59:1

~

Every man and woman has undeveloped strength undreamed of, until emergencies call it forth. Every one of us has been surprised at how much we can do and how well we can do it when we have to do it.

~

He … got the better of himself, and that's the best kind of victory one can wish for.

CERVANTES

My grace is sufficient for you, my power is made perfect in weakness.

2 CORINTHIANS 12:9

The men whom I have seen succeed have always been cheerful and hopeful, who went about their business with a smile on their faces, and took the changes and chances of this mortal life like men.

CHARLES KINGSLEY

He who is not prepared today will be less so tomorrow.

OVID

Rebellion against your handicaps gets you nowhere. Self-pity gets you nowhere. One must have the adventurous daring to accept oneself as a bundle of possibilities and undertake the most interesting game in the world – making the most of one's best.

HARRY EMERSON FOSDICK

~

Belief and faith in God do not bring instant solutions to all life's problems and obscurities; they do, however, equip us to deal with these.

~

Few things are impossible to diligence and skill.

SAMUEL JOHNSON

Everything is possible for him who believes.

MARK 9:23

It is the greatest of all mistakes to do nothing because you can only do a little. Do what you can.

SYDNEY SMITH

We do not know what is coming, but we do know Who is coming.

Though the fig tree does not bud and there are no grapes on the vines, though the olive crop fails and the fields produce no food, though there are no sheep in the pen and no cattle in the stalls, yet I will rejoice in the Lord, I will be joyful in God my Savior.

HABAKKUK 3:17

~

We must have perseverance and above all confidence in ourselves. We must believe that we are gifted for something ...

MARIE CURIE

Whatever your hand finds to do, do it with all your might ...

ECCLESIASTES 9:10

~

A man would do nothing, if he waited until he could do it so well that no one would find fault with what he has done.

JOHN HENRY NEWMAN

~

Where no plan is laid, where the disposal of time is surrendered merely to the chance of incidents, chaos will soon reign.

VICTOR HUGO

Say to those with fearful hearts, "Be strong, do not fear, your God will come."

ISAIAH 35:4

~

Difficulties are the things that show what men are.

EPICTETUS

~

Great works are performed not by strength but by perseverance.

SAMUEL JOHNSON

~

Nothing great was ever achieved without enthusiasm.

RALPH WALDO EMERSON

There are people who make no mistakes because they never try to do anything worth doing.

JOHANN WOLFGANG VON GOETHE

~

I have watched men climb up to success, hundreds of them, and of all the elements that are important for success, the most important is faith. No great thing comes to any man unless he has courage.

JAMES GIBBONS

~

I wait for the Lord, my soul waits, and in
his word I put my hope. My soul waits for the
Lord more than watchmen wait for the morning ...

PSALM 130:5, 6

If you think you'll lose,
you're lost,
For out in the world we find
success begins
with a person's faith;
it's all in the state of mind.
Life's battles don't always go
to the stronger or faster hand;
they go to the one who trusts in God
and always thinks, "I can."

ANONYMOUS

Our belief at the beginning of a doubtful undertaking is the one thing that insures the successful outcome of our venture.

WILLIAM JAMES

~

Blessed is the man who fears the Lord,
who finds great delight in his commands.
He will have no fear of bad news; his
heart is steadfast, trusting in the Lord.

PSALM 112:1, 7

~

The difference between perseverance and obstinacy is that one comes from a strong will, and the other from a strong won't.

HENRY WARD BEECHER

If a man measures life by what others do for him, he is apt to be disappointed; but if he measures life by what he does for others, there is no time for despair.

WILLIAM JENNINGS BRYAN

~

When I said, "My foot is slipping," your love, O Lord, supported me. When anxiety was great within me, your consolation brought joy to my soul.

PSALM 94:18, 19

~

Use what talents you possess; the woods would be very silent if no birds sang there except those that sang best.

HENRY VAN DYKE

In the long run, men hit only what they aim at. Therefore ... they had better aim at something high.

Henry David Thoreau

With man this is impossible, but with God all things are possible.

Matthew 19:26

It is true that we shall not be able to reach perfection, but in our struggle toward it we shall strengthen our characters and give stability to our ideas ...

Confucius

It may be that God allows problems and trials in our lives in order to lead us to serious self-examination so that we may surrender ourselves to him again.

WILLIE JONKER

~

That the circumstances of my life are what they are today, and not what they were yesterday or what they may be tomorrow – this is fraught with meaning. It is indeed part of God's great plan.

JOHAN HEYNS

~

Doing little things with a strong desire to please God makes them really great.

ST. FRANCIS DE SALES

Whatever you do, work at it with all your heart, as working for the Lord ...

COLOSSIANS 3:23

To pray together, in whatever tongue or ritual, is the most tender brotherhood of hope and sympathy that men can contract in this life.

MADAME DE STAËL

The weakest among us has a gift, however seemingly trivial, which is peculiar to him and, if worthily used, will be a gift also to his race.

JOHN RUSKIN

If you do not see your way clear to face the week or month ahead, live one day at a time. Tomorrow is another day.

~

Christians should be able to escape from the vicious circle of negative thoughts. If I know that God loves me just as I am, I should be able to accept it and also love myself.

~

Public opinion is a weak tyrant compared with our own private opinion. What a man thinks of himself, that it is what determines, or rather indicates, his fate.

HENRY DAVID THOREAU

Whatever is worth doing at all, is worth doing well.

PHILIP DORMER STANHOPE

Finish each day and be done with it. You have done what you could; some blunders no doubt crept in; forget them as soon as you can. Tomorrow is a new day; you shall begin it well and serenely.

RALPH WALDO EMERSON

The Lord's unfailing love
surrounds the man who trusts in him.

PSALM 32:10

Who of you by worrying can add a single hour to his life?

MATTHEW 6:27

~

There are but two ways which lead to great aims and achievements – energy and perseverance. Energy is a rare gift ... But perseverance lies within the affordings of everyone, its power increases with its progress, and it but rarely misses its aim.

JOHANN WOLFGANG VON GOETHE

~

Do not pray for easy lives; pray to be stronger men. Do not pray for tasks equal to your powers; pray for powers equal to your tasks ...

PHILLIP BROOKS

The world is round and the place which may
seem like the end may also be only the beginning.

IVY BAKER PRIEST

Truly lonely is the person who cannot open up his heart to others,
and who finds that others do not open up their hearts to him.

JOHAN HEYNS

God … comforts us in all our troubles,
so that we can comfort those in any trouble with
the comfort we ourselves have received from God.

2 CORINTHIANS 1:3, 4

One of the most tragic things I know about human nature is that all of us tend to put off living. We are all dreaming of some magical rose garden over the horizon – instead of enjoying the roses that are blooming outside our windows today.

DALE CARNEGIE

~

Life was meant to be lived, and curiosity must be kept alive. One must never, for whatever reason, turn one's back on life.

ELEANOR ROOSEVELT

~

God is in control of my life.
And when I cannot or will not continue
myself, He can and He will.
Hold on to life!
Hold on to hope!
Hold on to God!
And one day you will again see the light.

I. L. DE VILLIERS

~

When you become quiet before God, you realise that He is always there to support you. Then you will also be able to deal with your fear and worry.

I will not permit any man to narrow and degrade my soul by making me hate him.

BOOKER T. WASHINGTON

~

God is faithful; he will not let you be tempted beyond what you can bear. But when you are tempted, he will also provide a way out so that you can stand up under it.

1 CORINTHIANS 10:13

~

When love and skill work together, expect a masterpiece.

JOHN RUSKIN

~

I rejoice in life for its own sake. Life is no brief candle to me. It is a sort of splendid torch which I got hold of for a moment, and I want to make it burn as brightly as possible before turning it over to future generations.

GEORGE BERNARD SHAW

There is no road too long to the man who advances deliberately and without undue haste; there are no honors too distant to the man who prepares himself for them with patience.

JEAN DE LA BRUYÈRE

Man has survived everything, and we have only survived it on our optimism, and optimism means faith in ourselves, faith in the everydayness of our lives, faith in our universal qualities, and above all, faith in love.

EDWARD STEICHEN

~

Consider it pure joy, my brothers, whenever you face trials of many kinds, because you know that the testing of your faith develops perseverance. Perseverance must finish its work so that you may be mature and complete, not lacking anything.

JAMES 1:2, 3

~

Life is something like this trumpet. If you don't put anything in it you don't get anything out. And that's the truth.

W. C. Handy

Don't let life discourage you; everyone who got where he is had to begin where he was.

Richard L. Evans

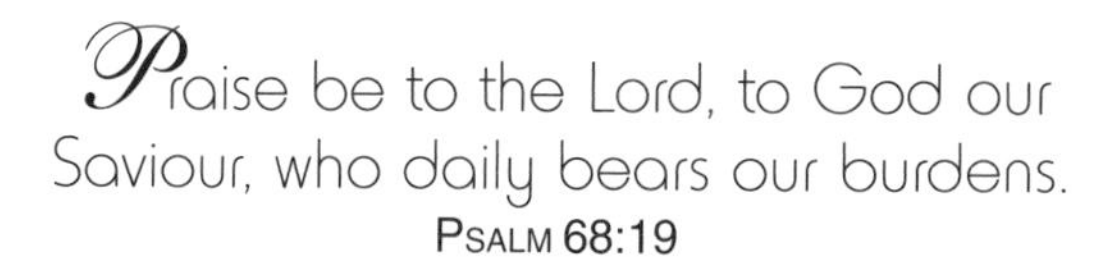

Praise be to the Lord, to God our Saviour, who daily bears our burdens.

Psalm 68:19

You should first make peace with God, with yourself and with your circumstances before you can start a meaningful relationship with others.

WILLIE VAN WYK

~

The best cure for worry, depression, melancholy, brooding, is to sally deliberately forth and try to lift with one's sympathy the gloom of somebody else.

ARNOLD BENNETT

~

A man should never be ashamed to say he has been wrong, which is but saying in other words that he is wiser today than he was yesterday.

ALEXANDER POPE

The Lord is a refuge for the oppressed, a stronghold in times of trouble. Those who know your name will trust in you, for you, Lord, have never forsaken those who seek you.

PSALM 9:9, 10

~

Live all you can; it's a mistake not to. It doesn't so much matter what you do in particular so long as you have your life. If you haven't had that what *have* you had?

HENRY JAMES

~

The most drastic and usually the most effective remedy for fear is direct action.

WILLIAM BURNHAM

In our sorrow we so easily forget that our God is still the same God who, throughout history, has always broken down strongholds of misery and wretchedness.

WILLIE JONKER

~

It need not be of the greatest importance what age I reach or how long I live, but rather how I live.

JOHAN HEYNS

~

Be strong and courageous. Do not be afraid or terrified because of them, for the Lord your God goes with you; he will never leave you nor forsake you.

DEUTERONOMY 31:6

What you think of yourself is much more important than what others think of you.

SENECA

The world is moving so fast these days that the man who says it can't be done is generally interrupted by someone doing it.

ELBERT HUBBARD

Come to me, all you who are weary and burdened, and I will give you rest. For my yoke is easy and my burden is light.

MATTHEW 11:28, 30

Those who attempt to search into the majesty of God will be overwhelmed with its glory.

Thomas à Kempis

~

I have set the Lord always before me. Because he is at my right hand, I will not be shaken.

Psalm 16:8

~

Write it on your heart that every day is the best day in the year.

Ralph Waldo Emerson

~

I can do everything through him who gives me strength.
PHILIPPIANS 4:13

~

God in Christ has taken all our anxieties onto Him and that is why we may leave our deepest fears to Him and rest assured that we are safe in the hands of God.
WILLIE JONKER

~

I am not bound to win but I am bound to be true. I am not bound to succeed but I am bound to live up to what light I have. I must stand with anybody that stands right: stand with him while he is right and part with him when he goes wrong.
ABRAHAM LINCOLN

Self-knowledge is best learned, not by contemplation, but action. Strive to do your duty and you will soon discover of what stuff you are made.

JOHANN WOLFGANG VON GOETHE

Bring your problems to God – He is going to be awake all night anyway.

Nothing will ever be attempted if all possible objections must be first overcome.

SAMUEL JOHNSON

The art of living successfully consists of being able to hold two opposite ideas in tension at the same time: first, to make long-term plans as if we were going to live forever; and, second, to conduct ourselves daily as if we were going to die tomorrow.

SYDNEY HARRIS

~

Never lose an opportunity of seeing anything that is beautiful; for beauty is God's handwriting – a wayside sacrament.

RALPH WALDO EMERSON

~

To get out of a difficulty, go through it.

SAMUEL EASTON

To be of use in this world is the only way to be happy.

HANS CHRISTIAN ANDERSON

~

Do not be terrified; do not be afraid of them. The Lord your God, who is going before you, will fight for you ...

DEUTERONOMY 1: 29, 30

~

People are always blaming their circumstances for what they are. I don't believe in circumstances. The people who get on in this world are the people who get up and look for the circumstances they want, and if they can't find them, make them.

GEORGE BERNARD SHAW

As Christians we are sometimes afraid, yet we always know who our Father is; and we believe that God surrounds us with his love amidst our fear.

~

Whatever you are by nature, keep to it; never desert your line of talent. Be what nature intended you for, and you will succeed.

SYDNEY SMITH

~

You came near when I called you, and you said, "Do not fear." O Lord, you took up my case; you redeemed my life.

LAMENTATIONS 3:57, 58

Do not wait for extraordinary circumstances to do good actions: try to use ordinary situations.

JEAN PAUL RICHTER

And only when we are no longer afraid do we begin to live in every experience, painful or joyous; to live in gratitude for every moment, to live abundantly.

DOROTHY THOMPSON

Every individual has a place to fill in the world, and is important in some respect, whether he chooses to be so or not.

NATHANIEL HAWTHORNE

The Lord bless you and keep you;
the Lord make his face shine upon you
and be gracious to you;
the Lord turn his face toward you
and give you peace.
NUMBERS 6:24-26

~

Prayer is the peace of our spirit,
the stillness of our thoughts, the evenness
of our recollection, the sea of our
meditation, the rest of our cares,
and the calm of our tempest.
JEREMY TAYLOR

Man needs, for his happiness, not only the enjoyment of this or that, but hope and enterprise and change.

BERTRAND RUSSELL

Until you know that life is interesting – and find it so – you haven't found your soul.

GEOFFREY FISHER

It is meditation that leads us in spirit into the hallowed solitudes wherein we find God alone – in peace, in calm, in silence, in recollection.

J. CRASSET

Love is an image of God, and not a lifeless image, but the living essence of the divine nature which beams full of all goodness.

MARTIN LUTHER

Let the Divine Mind flow through your mind, and you will be happier. I have found the greatest power in the world in the power of prayer. There is no shadow of doubt of that. I speak from my own experience.

CECIL B. DE MILLE

To accept what you are is to be content, and contentment is the greatest wealth. To work with patience is to gather power. To surrender to the Eternal flow is to be completely present.

VIMALIA MCCLURE

Our way is not soft grass, it's a mountain path with lots of rocks. But it goes upwards, forward, toward the sun.

Dr. Ruth Westheimer

I believe that basically people are people – but it is our differences which charm, delight, and frighten us.

Agnes Newton Keith

There is no law which lays down that you must smile! But you can make a gift of your smile; you can be the heaven of kindness in your family.

Pope John Paul

What do we live for, if it is not to
make life less difficult for each other?

George Eliot

A kind heart is a fountain of gladness, making
everything in its vicinity freshen into smiles.

Washington Irving

All who would win joy, must share it –
happiness was born a twin.

Lord Byron

The best cure for worry, depression, melancholy, brooding, is to go deliberately forth and try to lift with one's sympathy the gloom of somebody else.

ARNOLD BENNETT

Do all the good you can,
by all the means you can,
in all the ways you can,
in all the places you can,
to all the people you can,
as long as ever you can.

JOHN WESLEY

And my God will meet all your needs
according to his glorious riches in Christ Jesus.

PHILIPPIANS 4:19

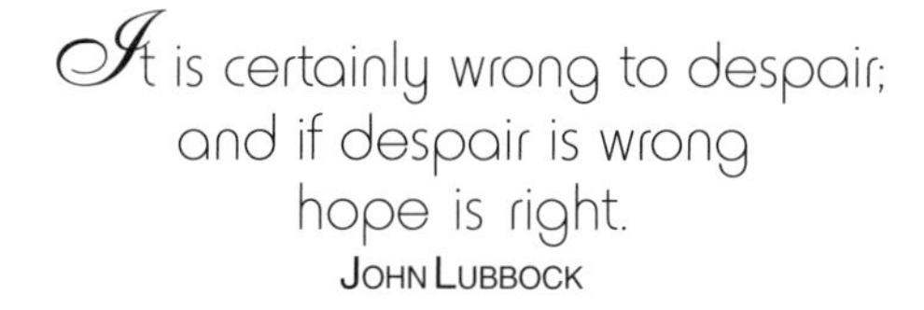

It is certainly wrong to despair;
and if despair is wrong
hope is right.

JOHN LUBBOCK

A simple, childlike faith in a Divine Friend solves
all the problems that come to us by land or sea.

HELEN KELLER

Consider it pure joy, my brothers, whenever you face trials of many kinds, because you know that the testing of your faith develops perseverance.

JAMES 1:2-3

Doubt is the vestibule which all must pass before they can enter the temple of wisdom.

CHARLES CALEB COLTON

One who fears, limits his activities. Failure is only the opportunity to more intelligently begin again.

HENRY FORD

Faith is trust.
By faith I mean a trust
in God's unknown,
unfelt, untried goodness
and mercy.

MARTIN LUTHER

~

But the eyes of the Lord are on those who fear him,
on those whose hope is in his unfailing love.

PSALM 33:18

Cheerfulness is the atmosphere in which all things thrive.

JEAN PAUL RICHTER

God has two dwellings: one in heaven
and the other in a meek and thankful heart.
IZAAK WALTON

But seek first his kingdom and his righteousness,
and all these things will be given to you as well.
Therefore do not worry about tomorrow, for tomorrow will
worry about itself. Each day has enough trouble of its own.
MATTHEW 6:33-34

To be trusted is a greater compliment than to be loved.
GEORGE MACDONALD

Our determination to imitate Christ should be such that we have no time for other matters.

ERASMUS

Whoever is happy will make others happy too. He who has courage and faith will never perish in misery.

ANNE FRANK

Be strong and courageous. Do not be afraid or discouraged.

1 CHRONICLES 22:13

Happy times and bygone days are never lost – in truth, they grow more wonderful within the heart that keeps them.

KAY ANDREW

God is our refuge and strength, an ever-present help in trouble.

PSALM 46:1

We attract hearts by the qualities we display; we retain them by the qualities we possess.

SCAD

Respect is appreciation of the separateness of the other person, of the ways in which he or she is unique.

ANNIE GOTTLIEB

~

The Lord your God is with you, he is mighty to save.
He will take great delight in you,
he will quiet you with his love,
he will rejoice over you with singing.

ZEPHANIAH 3:17

~

Human beings, by changing the inner attitudes of their minds, can change the outer aspects of their lives.

WILLIAM JAMES

I realized the problem was me and
nobody could change me except myself.

John Petworth

Guidance means that I can count on God.
Commitment means that God can count on me.

Anonymous

Stand firm in the faith; be men of
courage; be strong. Do everything in love.

1 Corinthians 16:13-14